MW01274007

ADVENTURES OF Milo

Jungle Dog of Devotees

BHAKTI LALITĀ DEVĪ DĀSĪ

Acknowledgments

Good teamwork made the production of this book possible. Special appreciations go out to Śrīla Bhakti Bimal Avadhūt Mahārāj (Russia) for his enthusiasm to facilitate this and hundreds of other devotional projects for the service of our divine masters. To Śrīla B.R. Madhusūdan Mahārāj (U.K./Kenya/India) for all of the the final proofreading with Lalitā Mādhava Prabhu (U.K.), who especially helped with the Devanāgarī (Sanskrit). Many thanks to Michael Dolan/B.V. Mahāyogi (U.S.A./Mexico) and Alwarnāth Prabhu (U.S.A.) for their help with the proofreading and editorial work; and to my very first volunteer Jessica Said Flick/Jaśodā Devī Dāsī (Hawaii, U.S.A.) for her fine input and the initial proofreading; to Gaurāṅga Das Prabhu (Brazil) for his support; to Pāvan Kṛṣṇa Prabhu (Russia) for all of our amazing artwork; Gaurahari Das of *the*BookDesigners for the book cover and layout design and to Sasa Hasid RA/Śambhunāth Prabhu (U.S.A.) for his magic touch with all of the technical formatting, programming and production.

Preface

Based on a true story, *Adventures of Milo: Jungle Dog of Devotees* takes its readers on a spiritual journey: an adorable Thai jungle dog by great fortune is rescued and adopted by a group of sādhus (Vaiṣṇava monks and devotees), and with the power of their love and affection his soul advances towards a higher prospect, leading to a life of loving pastimes with Divinity.

The essence of the *Adventures of Milo* is comprised of spiritual substance and ontological truths that spring from the ancient yet timeless culture and traditions of the Vedas—truths of revealed philosophy that transcend religion and the time and space of this objective world. While the simplicity of this story makes it especially suitable for young readers, it is intended for readers from any age group. The spiritual component of the tale imbues it with a universal application that is without regard for any sectarian concern. It is thus capable of appealing to the hearts of all those who are open to receiving its all-embracing message, irrespective of one's particular belief system or philosophy. At the very least, it may offer readers an invitation to the educational opportunity of experiencing a culture and philosophy that could potentially broaden and enrich their outlook on life.

This is not the first time that a humble dog received such grace from the Lord and His devotees. In the *Śrī Chaitanya-charitāmṛta,* the biography of Śrī Caitanya Mahāprabhu composed by Śrīla Kṛṣṇadāsa Kavirāj, we find some precedent for the *Adventures of Milo*. Kavirāj Goswāmī describes the story of a dog who accompanied Śivānanda Sena and a group of devotees on their pilgrimage to Jagannātha Purī in India. This dog was so fortunate that after reaching Purī, seeing the lotus feet of Mahāprabhu, and receiving some coconut from His hand, he was liberated and went directly to the spiritual world.

Our Milo wandered off into eternity before sunrise on the full solar eclipse day, 21 August 2017, leaving us with a mixture of heartbreak and loss, and ultimately celebration for his bright future and hopeful prospect.

As a participant in his adventures, I felt compelled to share his spiritually uplifting story, which at the same time served as a creative outlet for my heartache. It was enlivening and therapeutic to write it all down while observing how Milo's life wondrously threaded together. In my own expounding and finding closure to his story, I concluded it with Milo achieving the ideal set of circumstances for which I myself aspire: from being an object of affection to the devotees to receiving the immense grace needed to proceed in the direction of Goloka Vrindavan, the land of Śrī Kṛṣṇa.

For our artwork, instead of illustrating Milo and all of us into cartoon-type characters, we opted for using painted photographs by our ever-talented artist and photographer Pāvan Kṛṣṇa Prabhu. This allows our readers to see the real Milo, all of us real-life characters, and actual scenes from the holy place of Gupta-Govardhan 'captured in action' (a touch of digital enhancement was made to two of our paintings: Milo as a puppy and our Gaura-pūrṇimā kīrtan).

Humbly bowing down to my divine master, Śrīla Bhakti Sundar Govinda Dev-Goswāmī Mahārāj, and on behalf of all of the team, we wish our readers a pleasant, entertaining and inspiring read.

Finding Milo

The ancient kingdom of Siam is today called Thailand. Some time ago, in the eastern region of Thailand not far from Cambodia and the ruins of Angkor Wat, there lived a humble gardener named Samrit. Samrit was a poor and honest man who was always content with what little came to him.

One day, in search of a better means to support his family, Samrit travelled to the northern territory previously called the Lanna Kingdom, the 'kingdom of a million rice fields' where elephants still roam the jungle today. There, he soon found work as caretaker for a few overgrown acres of jungle land that included a disused school. A world renowned Sanskrit professor, who was a leader in the field of Vedic ritual studies,

had settled and built a college there, where his students could learn the language of the ancient mantras of the Vedas. The professor's dying wish was that Sanskrit would always be chanted in this place.

Samrit looked after the garden, cutting back weeds, maintaining the old schoolhouse, and chasing away snakes that sometimes crossed the little stream in the back of the school. One afternoon, upon his returning to the grounds, Samrit stumbled upon a little puppy romping about aimlessly back and forth across the old road. Samrit could see the pup had no home, as he was unkempt and hungry. The little puppy looked up at the gardener with shining eyes, a black button nose, and a bright pink tongue. The puppy was fluffy and playful. He had a spring in his step and an extra pad on his back paws. There was no way to help the little lost dog in the road, so Samrit decided to take him back home.

As he gave him some food, Samrit thought of a name. "His name should be Milo," he thought, since the pup's fur coat resembled the colour of chocolate (the powdered chocolate drink Milo). And so it was that the little puppy was christened 'Milo,' and that was the pup's name from then on.

Happy Jungle Living

Milo loved the jungle life, and within a short time the little pup grew into a handsome young dog. All the neighbouring locals knew of Milo and had great affection for him. They would call out his name as they drove by, sometimes stopping to shake his paw. Naughty Milo loved to chase after motorbikes, always giving the drivers a good scare.

Milo was free to come and go as he pleased, and he knew every nook and cranny of the surrounding area. He was adventurous, running through the back jungles of bamboo, palm trees, and elephant grass, and jumping across streams. He was always full of dirt and tiny burrs from the bushes, and sometimes even flowers clung to his fur, making him look decorated.

Every time Samrit bathed him, Milo would immediately roll around in the dust just as an elephant does. It was impossible to keep him clean, and oftentimes Milo's fluffy coat would attract fleas and ticks. Although Samrit was able to provide food and shelter, he did not have the means to take proper care of a jungle dog and could hardly pay for a veterinary doctor, so he began to worry about what to do if Milo were to fall ill. In any case, Milo was a constant companion to the humble gardener, and Samrit would always take the time to patiently remove any ticks before they caused the dog any harm.

Meeting Goswāmī

As the school's property had been vacant for some time, Samrit lived alone in the jungle with his only companion, Milo, until his luck changed.

One day a very intelligent sādhu, a Vaiṣṇava sannyāsī (monk) named Goswāmī, and a group of Kṛṣṇa-loving devotees arrived from various countries to visit the land. They were effulgent and in a happy mood and were looking for a suitable place to start a temple for Lord Girirāj-Govardhan, a unique form of the Lord from Govardhan Mountain in India. Samrit and Milo warmly welcomed the group and took everyone on a tour of the property. The grounds were swept clean and nicely cared for. Bamboo stalks stood tall and plentiful, trees grew laden with tropical fruits, and colourful flowers decorated the forestation, emitting a lovely fragrance all around.

Flowing along the bottom of the property line was a small stream in the shape of an Om, the first syllable of the Vedic mantras. Flying squirrels flew from tree to tree, peeking down at everyone with their little aviator eyes, and living amongst the trees was a wide variety of birds, an indication of auspiciousness and the artistic nature of Divinity.

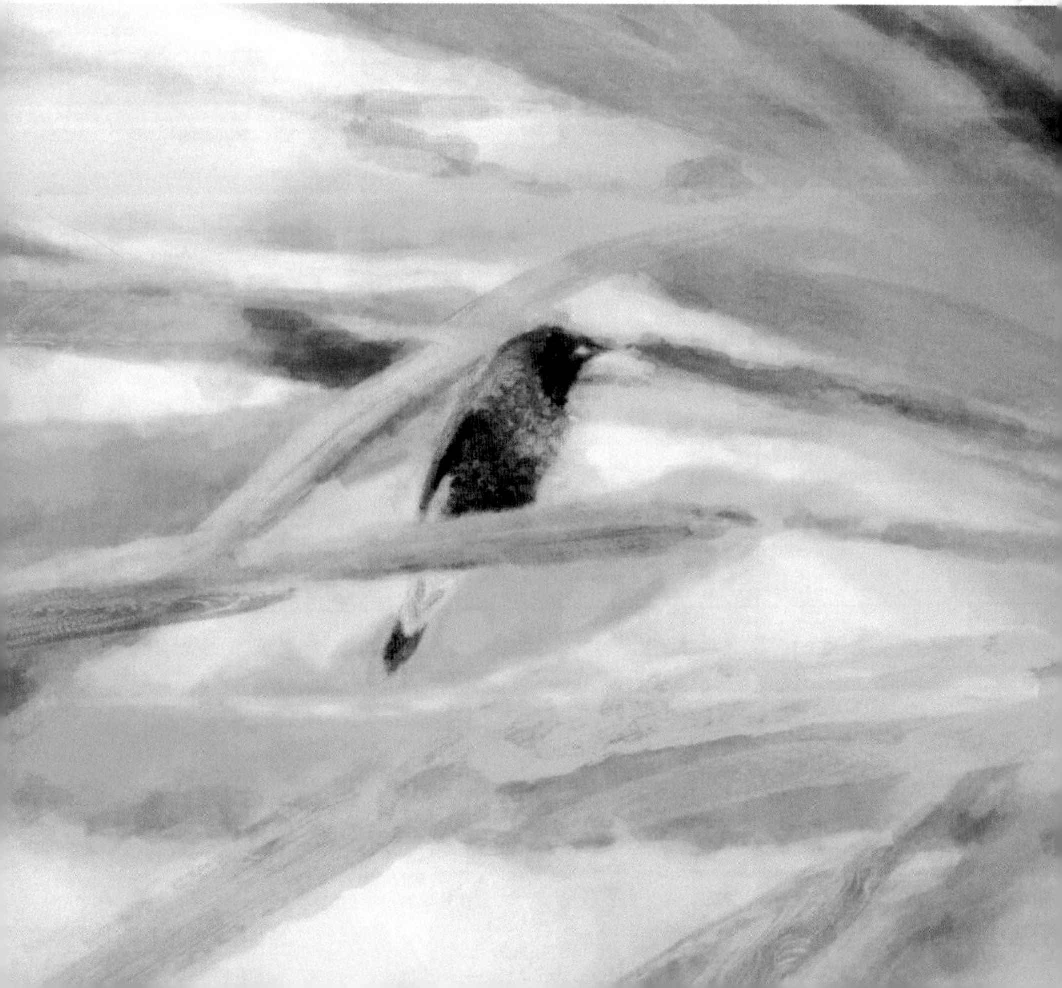

वयांसि तद्व्याकरणं विचित्रं
मनुर्मनीषा मनुजो निवासः ।
गन्धर्वविद्याधरचारणाप्सरः
स्वरस्मृतीरसुरानीकवीर्यः ।।

vayāṁsi tad-vyākaraṇaṁ vichitraṁ
manur manīṣā manujo nivāsaḥ
gandharva-vidyādhara-chāraṇāpsaraḥ
svara-smṛtīr asurānīka-vīryaḥ

(Śrīmad Bhāgavatam 2.1.36)

"All things great and wondrous show the beauty and power of the Lord. His art is seen in all the colourful birds, the sight of which reminds us of His perfect beauty. His home is found in the hearts all of humankind. His musical rhythms are heard in the songs of the holy angels, reminding us of the divine flute-song of Śrī Kṛṣṇa. And His awesome might is seen in the destructive wars of the titans."

Living With the Saints

After some time, the visiting monks began enquiring into purchasing the land that had once been a Sanskrit school as the group indeed felt it to be a perfect place to settle. It was lush and spacious, and the stream brought fresh water, which was cooling in the summertime. Samrit and Milo were happy to know that the wishes of the old owner would come true as, once again, Sanskrit mantras would vibrate through the bamboo forest in the jungle.

During the time it took to acquire the land, Goswāmī would often come by to spend time there in meditation. He knew many Sanskrit verses and would chant them out loud, just as the late professor had wished for. Samrit was happy that he would be kept on as the groundskeeper and that the land would get better care with the new owners. He and Milo would finally have some company.

And so it was that Goswāmī and Milo quickly became good friends. One day, Goswāmī had a talk with the jungle dog. After all, dogs sometimes like to make trouble, and with monks meditating quietly at the ashram, there might be a problem. Goswāmī asked Milo very seriously if he would like to stay on the land when it became a temple.

Milo looked up at him with joy in his eyes and wagged his tail. Goswāmī had only one condition: that Milo live like a brahmachārī, a chaste and celibate student, as were all who lived in the ashram. Milo enthusiastically wagged his tail in agreement and smiled. By this time Milo was no longer a puppy. He had become a bit older with the years and his two bottom teeth were missing, so he had a funny little smile, but his days of chasing after strange animals in the jungle were over. He understood perfectly and happily agreed to live a life of service. Everything was in harmony.

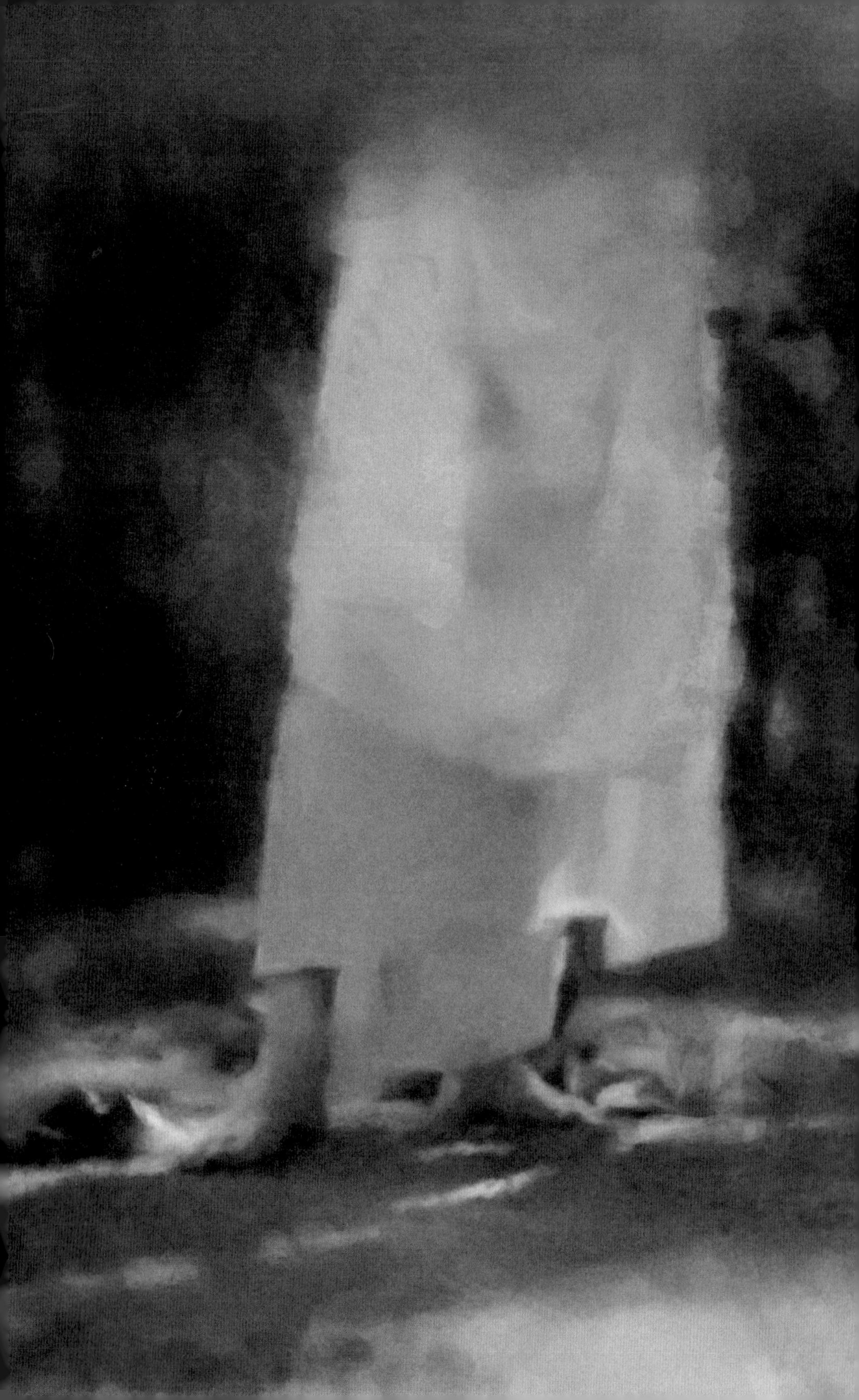

Milo in Danger

A few days later, however, Milo suddenly fell sick. He had a high fever and his nose was warm and dry. Samrit was beside himself and had no other way but to simply pray that Goswāmī would come back and take Milo to get some help. Samrit needed to go out, and so he gently tied Milo under a shady tree so that he would not wander off as usual. That day Goswāmī did visit the property, and when he saw Milo, he noted that he was just lying there unresponsively, unlike his usual self. He wasn't sure what to do at that moment and Samrit was not there to clarify, so Goswāmī decided that it was best not to intervene, and he simply left, a bit perplexed. The next morning Goswāmī thought to himself: "Could Samrit have tied Milo up for me to take him to the animal hospital?" Goswāmī decided to go back and check up on Milo. Again not finding Samrit, Goswāmī took Milo to a devotee veterinarian named Dhaniṣṭhā. Milo spent nearly one month in the hospital, and with the care of Dhaniṣṭhā he recovered from what ended up being a tick-borne disease. From then on, Milo stayed with Goswāmī and the devotees, and they all assisted in taking good care of him.

In time for the celebration of Śrī Gaura-pūrṇimā, the appearance day anniversary of the Prema Avatār, Śrī Gaurāṅga Mahāprabhu, Girirāj-Govardhan was brought to His new land. Girirāj was accompanied by His many devotees, who blew conch-shells, chanted, and danced with joyful hearts in celebration of this auspicious time. A temporary temple room had been created, and a new altar decorated with flowers and flags had been prepared for Girirāj. As the Lord was placed on His new asana (throne), at that exact moment all of the birds in the surrounding area began to sing at once. The kokilas, swallows, babblers, warblers, partridges, and owls each began to sing their own melodious songs. Even the pigeons, crows, and roosters each sang their unique songs together in unison. It was an auspicious moment indeed!

Temple Life

Samrit continued to garden part time for the temple, and the other part of his time was spent gardening for a neighbouring hotel. He moved down the road from the temple, and Milo would sometimes stay with Samrit, but he mostly spent his time on the property with the devotees. Milo was happy to live in the company of sādhus, those who live virtuous lives in accordance with their understanding of timeless spiritual truth. He spent his days and nights listening to the kīrtans, the devotional songs glorifying various manifestations of the Lord, and to the Vedic scriptures that were recited and discussed by the assembled devotees.

सतां प्रसङ्गान्मम वीर्यसंविदो
भवन्ति हृत्कर्णरसायनाः कथाः ।
तज्जोषणादाश्वपवर्गवर्त्मनि
श्रद्धा रतिर्भक्तिरनुक्रमिष्यति ।।

satāṁ prasaṅgān mama vīrya-
saṁvido bhavanti hṛt-karṇa-rasāyanāḥ
kathāḥ taj-joṣaṇād āśv apavarga-
vartmani śraddhā ratir bhaktir
anukramiṣyati

(Śrīmad-Bhāgavatam 3.25.25)

"By the association of the sadhus, saintly persons, discussions revealing the super-glories of the Supreme Absolute Truth that are nectar to the ear and heart take place. Continue affectionately in this way, and quickly you will first gain faith, then heart's devotion, and finally divine love or prema-bhakti will graciously appear within your heart. Associate with the sādhus and follow their directives, and then you will understand everything. Why? Because the sādhus are always trying to satisfy the Lord, and you can see how they satisfy Him by having their association. If they are affectionate to you, they will give that same quality of consciousness to you and you will easily get His mercy. Whoever follows them reaches the lotus feet of the Lord very quickly."

Merciful Maha-prasadam

Milo would attend the traditional morning and evening worship of Girirāj and circumambulate the holy Tulasī tree, and when he thought that no one would notice, he would circumambulate Girirāj's altar inside the temple room too. Although he struggled with his vegetarianism, which was mandatory in the ashram, Milo loved the various food offerings made to Girirāj, especially anything that contained cheese.

One day, Avadhūt, the big, jolly, generous-hearted monk who was the inspiration behind the establishing of the temple, arrived after going on pilgrimage in India. He brought with him from Jagannāth Puri some

of Lord Jagannāth's mahā-prasādam, the food offerings that Lord Jagannāth accepts, which is non-different from the Lord Himself. It is said that only souls who have the grace of Kṛṣṇa can receive such remnants. By honoring such nectarean mahā-prasādam, one is freed from mundane materialistic contamination and great spiritual fortune is ensured. So Avadhūt distributed this wonderful mahā-prasādam to everyone, and gave a large piece to a grateful Milo as well.

কৃষ্ণ বড় দয়াময়, করবিারে জহি্বা জয়,
স্বপ্রসাদ অন্ন দলি ভাই ।
সহৈ অন্নামৃত পাও, রাধাকৃষ্ণ-গুণ গাও,
প্রমে ডাক চতৈন্য-নতিাই ।।

kṛṣṇa baḍa dayāmaya, karibāre jihvā jaya, sva-prasāda anna dila bhāi sei annāmṛta pāo, rādhā-kṛṣṇa-guṇa gāo, preme ḍāko chaitanya-nitāi

(Śrīla Bhakti Vinod Ṭhākura)

"O brothers and sisters! Kṛṣṇa is very merciful: to control the voracious tongue He has given us His remnants. Accept this nectarean food, sing the glories of Rādhā-Kṛṣṇa, and with love call out 'Chaitanya! Nitāi!'"

Hidden Govardhan Hill

Due to the potency of Girirāj's presence, an approximate twenty mile radius surrounding the temple became surcharged with auspiciousness. As a part of the infinite is also infinite, by bringing a part of Govardhan mountain to the temple, the area became Gupta-Govardhan, or Govardhan which is 'hidden' or non-seeable by ordinary vision. The main road to the temple, previously full of potholes, became nicely paved. Wealth and prosperity also came to all the residents there—rain fell abundantly upon the land which had become drought-ridden, and vegetation grew healthy and vibrant. The local people brought flowers from their trees for Girirāj, and they happily heard the transcendental sound vibrations of the kīr-tan, including the ceremonial conch-shell blowing at sunrise and sunset.

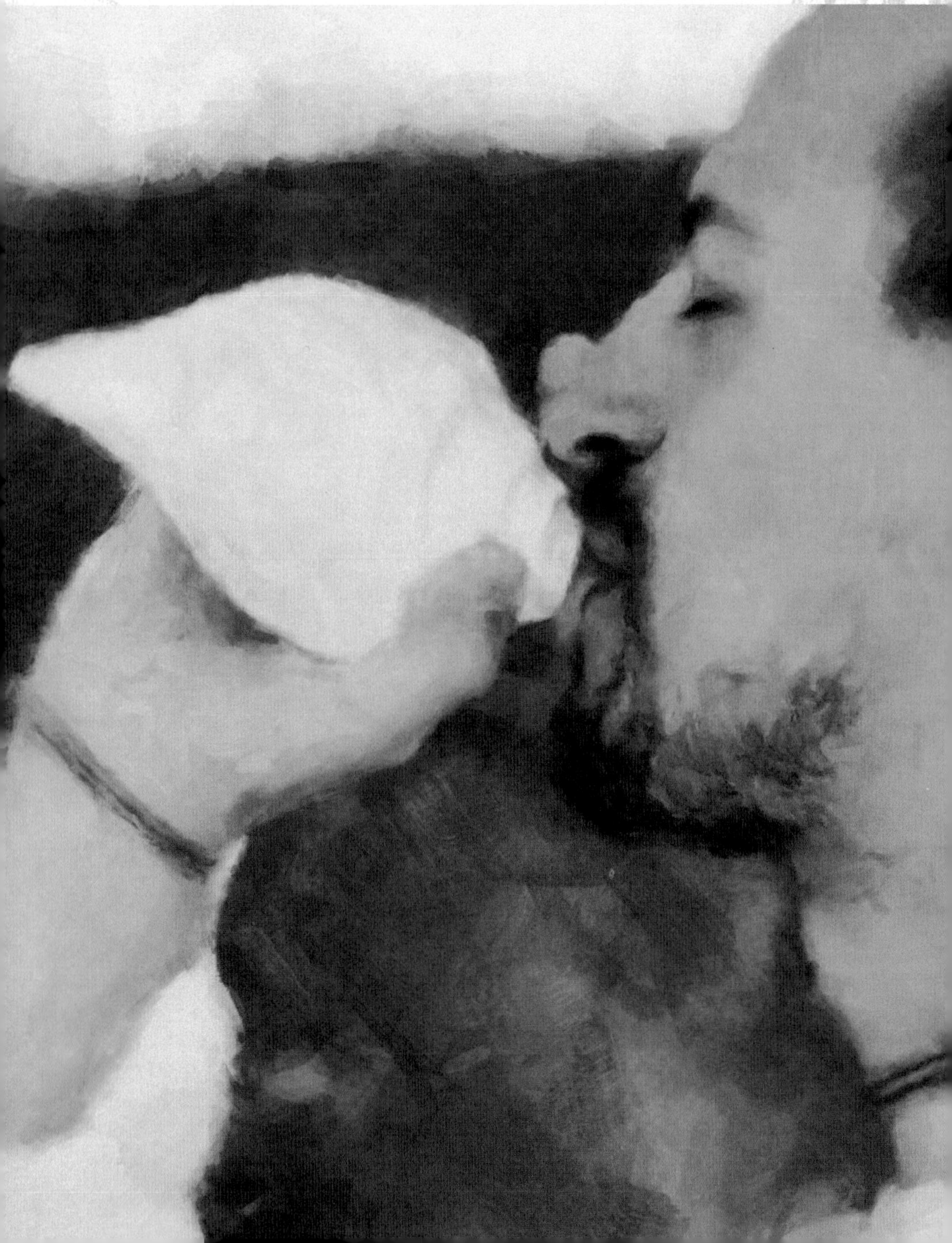

A Spark of Krsna's Splendour

Every day Milo went walking with the devotees of the temple, and he also rode around on motor scooters with them. Sometimes he rode balancing at the feet of the driver, while at other times he sat on the seat with his paws on the handlebars. Milo seemed to understand whatever anyone was saying to him in whatever language they were speaking, whether it was in Thai, English, Russian, or Chinese. And whenever he heard anyone talking about him, he became embarrassed and held his snout with his two front paws!

Overtime Milo developed a strong bond with one of the women in the ashram named Lalitā, who lived in the renounced order of life and wore the sacred saffron cloth. She would sing songs to Girirāj in the temple, and Milo would sit with her and listen. She would take Milo on long walks throughout the jungle and chant as they went. Although Milo had aged, he would still play like a pup. With a big grin on his face, he would gallop like a horse, cool off in puddles of muddy water, and roll around on his back, ever playful. Lalitā was charmed by Milo's lovable nature, but at the same time she understood from her spiritual master and the Bhagavad-gītā that 'all beautiful and glorious creations spring from but a spark of God's splendour'. She reflected that anything beautiful and adorable could be considered to represent Kṛṣṇa's opulence—even a dog.

A Reflection of the Absolute

The Lord has many different names related to His unlimited qualities and amorous pastimes—names like Gopāla, Govinda, Rāma, Śrī Madhusūdana, Giridhārī, Gopīnātha, and Madana-mohana. When you love someone, you may call them by many nicknames, and so it was that Lalitā assigned many nicknames to Milo, such as: 'Girirāj's-Lo', 'Smile-Lo', 'Love Puff', or just 'The Puff'. Lalitā intuited that not only nicknaming, but everything we find here in this relative world originates from and is a reflection of the Absolute.

Life Extension

As time passed, Milo experienced three more near-death events. In one incident he sustained a festering injury from a dogfight, in another he was nearly run over by a truck, and, lastly, he was stricken by an old-age-related illness. The devotees saved him each time, thereby extending his lifetime and allowing him to accumulate more and more sukṛti or personal spiritual fortune. Milo soon became increasingly humble in his old age as his doggie ego was deflating, and he wholly stopped fighting with other dogs. His heart became peaceful and he only wanted to stay in the temple, sometimes sitting alone in the back of the temple room gazing at Girirāj.

On the occasion of the fifth anniversary celebration of Gaura-pūrṇimā in Gupta-Govardhan, a big kīrtan took place and all of the assembled devotees were loudly chanting and dancing in a joyous festive mood. When the kīrtan reached a crescendo, Milo joined in and began happily barking, jumping up and down, and ecstatically wagging his tail in the middle of the festivities. Everybody laughed in delight to see this wonderful occurrence. It indeed seemed that Milo was internally experiencing the transcendental sound vibration of the mahā-mantra, and that the sound was penetrating his ears and entering into his soul.

हरे कृष्ण हरे कृष्ण कृष्ण कृष्ण हरे हरे हरे
राम हरे राम राम राम हरे हरे

hare kṛṣṇa hare kṛṣṇa, kṛṣṇa kṛṣṇa hare
hare hare rāma hare rāma, rāma rāma hare hare

शत्रुच्छेदैकमन्त्रं सकलमुपनिषद्वाक्यसम्पूज्यमन्त्रं
संसारोच्छेदमन्त्रं समुचिततमसः सङ्घनिर्याणमन्त्रम् ।
सर्वैश्वर्यैकमन्त्रं व्यसनभुजगसन्दष्टसन्त्राणमन्त्रं
जिह्वे श्रीकृष्णमन्त्रं जप जप सततं जन्मसाफल्यमन्त्रम् ।।

śatru-chchhedaika-mantraṁ sakalam upaniṣad-vākya-sampūjya-mantraṁ
saṁsārochchheda-mantraṁ samuchita-tamasaḥ saṅgha-niryāṇa-mantram
sarvaiśvaryaika-mantraṁ vyasana-bhujaga-sandaṣṭa-santrāṇa-mantraṁ
jihve śrī-kṛṣṇa-mantraṁ japa japa satataṁ janma-sāphalya-mantram

(Mukunda-mālā-stotra, by King Kulaśekhara, verse 31)

"O tongue, at every opportunity please chant the mantra that consists of the names of Lord Śrī Kṛṣṇa. This mantra is worshipped by the personified Upaniṣads, and it destroys all of the mind-created enemies, which, in the state of delusion, one imagines oneself to have. This mantra verily uproots the entire hypnotic dream of material existence and drives away all of the darkness brought about by ignoring one's true spiritual nature. Yet even during the duration of the wondrous universal dream, this mantra can award one incalculable prosperity as well as relief from the poisonous snake-bite of worldly miseries. It is the mantra par excellence for bestowing success in one's endeavours for divine self-realisation."

Final Farewells

By this time Milo had collected as much sukṛti as he possibly could in his dog body. The monsoon season was just around the corner and Lalitā would go traveling for several months during this period throughout the summer. On the morning of her departure, Milo could sense that she was leaving and didn't want to leave her side. When the car came to take her to the airport, he jumped into the car and refused to leave. Eventually, however, Milo relented and expressed his goodbyes, watching the car drive off into the distance. He remained in the good care of Samrit and the devotees, and especially enjoyed spending most of his time with Vāsudeva, a gentle young devotee from Ukraine, and Līlāvatī from China.

Milo could instinctively feel his time in this world waning away. The inevitable hour was approaching when he would transmigrate out of his dog body, thus ending his life-cycle as a dog. Milo went and bid his farewell to Samrit, and then he climbed up onto the temple construction site and gazed out into the sunset.

Retiring to the Jungle

Early before sunrise, a day when a full solar eclipse was due to take place, Milo paid his respects to the temple and wandered off quietly without anyone noticing. He didn't want to cause his loved ones any disturbance, so he found a secret hiding place and curled up in a secluded nook of the jungle. He slowly closed his eyes and breathed out all of his life-airs, thereby relinquishing all association and identification with his dog body.

न जायते म्रियते वा कदाचिन्
नायं भूत्वा भविता वा न भूयः ।
अजो नित्यः शाश्वतोऽयं पुराणो
न हन्यते हन्यमाने शरीरे ।।

na jāyate mriyate vā kadāchin
nāyaṁ bhūtvā bhavitā vā na bhūyaḥ
ajo nityaḥ śāśvato 'yaṁ purāṇo
na hanyate hanyamāne śarīre

(Bhagavad-gītā 2.20)

"The soul is neither born nor dies; it has neither been nor will it be created, because it is unborn and eternal. It is ever-youthful, yet primeval. It is not destroyed when the body is destroyed."

Surrender and Acceptance

Meanwhile, Lalitā had returned from her travels, and she learned of Milo's having disappeared while she was away. She felt that Milo had already left this world, but still she went in search of him. She searched through thickets of overgrown jungle in every area possible, realizing soon enough that Milo could not be found. Lalitā knew of the eternal spirit-self, she had faith in the Lord's protection, and she understood in principle that there was no need to lament. Still this loss affected her greatly and forced her to go deeper to a new level of surrender and acceptance.

In accordance with a certain Vedic tradition intended for the spiritual benefit of a departed soul, Lalitā asked a favour of a sannyāsi sādhu named Tīrtha in India, a brāhmaṇa priest who possessed the power to satisfy the Lord with mantras, prayers and sumptuous food preparations, then satisfy the sādhus and devotees with the mahā-prasādam, remnants of food offered to the Lord, in the name of the soul. Lalitā asked the sādhu if he would perform this service for Milo's benefit and he agreed to do so, choosing an auspicious time for the ceremony.

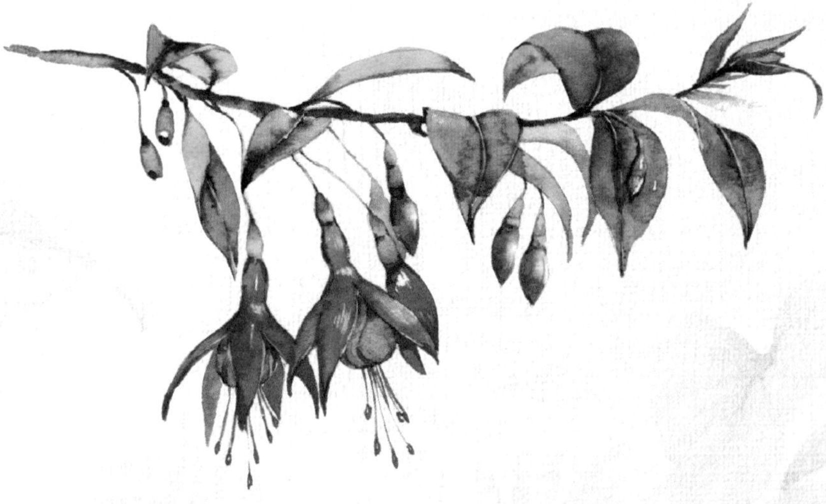

Descending Grace and Ascending Home

On the day of Govardhan-Pūjā, the worship of Govardhan Hill, big celebrations took place all over the world. There was a tremendous festival in Vrindavan, India, where Govardhan Hill is situated, and during the festivities there at the beautiful Śrīla Śrīdhar Swāmī Sevā Āśram, after satisfying Lord Anu Girirāj and the Vaiṣṇavas, the sādhu graciously summoned Milo's soul. He offered Milo a plate of Girirāj's mahā-prasādam, and that prasādam was transferred to him in the form of spiritually nourishing substance for Milo's soul.

By the association of the sādhus, the power of their affection, and the grace of Kṛṣṇa's holy names and His mahā-prasādam, one receives the good fortune to enter into the realm where the pastimes of Śrī Kṛṣṇa

are eternally taking place. From hidden Govardhan, to Govardhan in Vrindavan on Earth, Milo's bright future awaits him in his 'forever home' in the transcendental abode of Govardhan in the spiritual sky.

Information

facebook.com/TheisticMediaStudios

soundcloud.com/bhakti-lalita-devi

youtube.com/BhaktiLalitaDD

vk.com/bhakti_lalita

premadharma.org

Blddmorningclass@gmail.com

Made in the USA
Monee, IL
31 July 2021

74675833R00036